We Interrupt This Thought For An Important Senior Moment

Whimsical Musings,
Chuckles & Witticisms

Do not take this was given to me – Betty

Inspired by Faith

We Interrupt This Thought For An Important Senior Moment
ISBN 978-0-9977556-5-7

Published by Product Concept Mfg., Inc.
2175 N. Academy Circle #200, Colorado Springs, CO 80909

©2017 Product Concept Mfg., Inc. All rights reserved.

Written and Compiled by Patricia Mitchell
in association with Product Concept Mfg., Inc.

All scripture quotations are from the King James version
of the Bible unless otherwise noted.

Scriptures taken from the Holy Bible,
New International Version®, NIV®.
Copyright © 1973, 1978, 1984 by Biblica, Inc.™
Used by permission of Zondervan.
All rights reserved worldwide.
www.zondervan.com

Sayings not having a credit listed are contributed by writers
for Product Concept Mfg., Inc. or in a rare case,
the author is unknown.

The most wasted of all days
is one without laughter.

E. E. Cummings

So you might get this little book for someone much, *much* older than yourself? Or have you been noticing a few gray hairs and some of those "smile lines" in the bathroom mirror? Well, your secret is safe with us!

No matter where you are in that life stage we call "middle age" (and it's a long, long stage), you're bound to enjoy this collection of quips and quotes, chuckles and jokes, tongue-in-cheek musings and laugh-out-loud cartoons—all geared to those of us who have been around a while. Because we've learned how to take it all in stride, and we know that laughter makes us feel better— way better.

Go ahead and give yourself a lift (and that much, *much* older friend of yours, too) with a healthy and heart-happy dose of good, clean humor. Everyone could use a good laugh today!

It's Noticed

A store's credit card customer received a strongly worded "second notice" that her bill was overdue. In a panic, the customer went immediately to the store, paid the bill, and promised to pay more attention in the future.

"Oh," said the woman at the service desk, "we don't send out first notices any longer—we've found that second notices are much more effective."

Dream On!

One morning, the wife announced, "Last night I dreamed that you gave me a diamond bracelet for our thirtieth wedding anniversary tomorrow. What do you think that means?"

"You'll know tomorrow," said her husband with a smile.

The next day, he presented his wife with a small, beautifully wrapped gift. Eagerly, she opened it. Inside was a book entitled, *"The Meaning of Dreams."*

ID, Please

At the local diner, an elderly gent walked up to another senior who was putting on an overcoat. "Excuse me," the gent said, "but do you happen to be Mr. Gray?"

"No, I'm not Mr. Gray," the senior replied gruffly as he buttoned the garment.

"Well, as it happens, I am Mr. Gray, and that's his overcoat you're putting on."

Things you don't want to hear the surgeon mutter during a medical procedure:

- Concentration has always been one of my weak points.

- Hmmm…I'm never quite sure what to do at this point.

- I'm pretty new at this, guys.

- The lights are flickering—think we're about to have a power outage?

- Sure wish I hadn't left my glasses at home.

- Nurse, hand me that…uh…thingamajig.

- Oh no—someone tore out page 12 of the instruction manual!

- Huh…interesting. Never seen this before.

- Well, well, well…what have we here?

- Let's get this done pronto…the game's on TV in a couple hours.

- And they said this would be a simple operation.

- He shouldn't be waking up at this point— I'm not finished yet.

Your Attention, Please!

Mindful living is something most of us have tried, at least once. After considering a few inspirational quotes touting the benefits of paying attention to each moment, it's hard to disagree with the point. After all, what's not to like about remembering what we ate for dinner last night? About turning off autopilot and paying attention to what we're actually doing? About recalling crossing certain intersections on routes we travel every day? Or about saying with some degree of certainty that we did, indeed, pay the gas bill and call Aunt Susie?

So we determined we'd start paying attention, but then real life butted in. Too many things to do, too many places to be (usually all at one time) to ponder every itty bitty, routine task. Old habits took over, and once again we found ourselves falling into bed exhausted with little idea of precisely what it was that drained every ounce of our energy that day.

At a certain age, however, mindful living is thrust upon us, whether we like it or not. We have to pay attention—strict attention!—to what we're doing at any given moment. Why? Because if we don't, senior moments sprout like dandelions after a spring shower. We store the ice cream in the oven. We search frantically for our cell phone, holding it in our hand the whole time. We misplace the car keys, and sometimes even the car itself. (Yes, those car alarms aren't going off because a thief is trying to steal the car…they're going off because some wandering soul is trying to find the car.)

So forget about multi-tasking. One task and only one task is enough of us, thank you. And even that might require a short pause now and again to re-establish what it is we're trying to accomplish. Those occasions when our laser-focus carries us through with no major (or publically noticeable) lapse into senior moment-hood, then we can sit down, close our eyes, and do our best impression of serenity personified. We're not dozing, mind you, just experiencing the present moment to the fullest.

Tidbits of Truth

Everything has been said before, but since nobody's paying attention, we have to keep going back and saying everything all over again.

The good thing about egotists is that they aren't fixated on what everyone else is doing.

Knowledge is seeing that you're about to cross a one-way street. Wisdom is looking in both directions anyway.

A smile is a curve that sets many things straight.

If the grass is greener on the other side of the fence, you can be sure your neighbor's water bill is higher.

Don't sweat the petty things…and don't pet the sweaty things.

"My memory's not as sharp as it used to be. And in addition, my memory's not as sharp as it used to be."

Forget Something?

"The older Gus gets, the more forgetful he gets," complained a sales manager to one of his supervisors. "He left an hour ago to get sandwiches, and I bet he comes back empty-handed."

Just then, Gus burst into the office. "You'll never guess what happened!" he cried. "At the sandwich shop, I met old man Stevens, who hasn't bought from us in years. Well, we started talking, and the next thing you know, he gave me a million-dollar contract!"

"See, I told you," the sales manager said to the supervisor, "he forgot the sandwiches."

Worth Noting

To be seventy years young is sometimes far more cheerful and hopeful than to be forty years old.
Oliver Wendell Holmes

If wrinkles must be written upon our brows, let them not be written upon the heart. The spirit should never grow old.
James A. Garfield

What lies behind us and what lies before us are tiny matters compared to what lies within us.
Ralph Waldo Emerson

Do What?

Some people have a list of things-that-must-be-seen-and-done before they get to the Pearly Gates. So they plan and plot with meticulous care to make sure they will hit every destination, see each mind-blowing sight, and do all the out-of-the-ordinary activities they've ever fantasized about doing.

Now we're not talking about visiting a state park or big-city museum, or taking time out to enjoy the soothing sounds of nature. Small potatoes! No, we're talking about zip lining above the canopy of an Amazon rain forest, or gazing at the world from the top of Mount Everest.

Or doing a few of those things we used to sit in our office cubicle and dream about: Trekking across Europe hampered by nothing more than a lone backpack, a bottle of water, and a few energy bars. Going on a photo safari through an African jungle. Rappelling down a glacier in far northern Alaska. Bungee jumping from a biplane over a wide open field of wildflowers.

That kind of stuff. Big stuff.

But in retirement, when we could pursue those adventures we spent so much of our employer's time fantasizing about, we—those of us who have no to-do list—are entertaining other thoughts. Instead of the tiring (and pricey) business of actually going to exotic places and doing wild and crazy things, we realize that we're perfectly delighted to look at the photos that our thrill-seeking friends post online.

We're truly amazed! We're honestly impressed! We gladly press "like," and then do what we really want to do—putter in the garden, finish a novel, walk our furry, four-footed housemates, take the grandkids to the zoo. It's just the way we are.

Of course, if you have a things-that-must-be-seen-and-done list, hey, go for it! You're the brave one, the one who does what it takes to make a dream come true. And know that the rest of us depend on you to open our minds to new worlds and perform all those daring deeds that are so, so cool, but the idea of ourselves actually being there? That doesn't last long enough to grab a pen and write it down.

Worth Noting

Grow old with me!
The best is yet to be.
Robert Browning

In the end,
it's not the years in your life that count.
It's the life in your years.
Abraham Lincoln

None are so old as those
who have outlived enthusiasm.
Henry David Thoreau

Birthdays are good for you!
The more you have, the longer you live!

The difference between then and now...

- Then, the time you took to get ready for a special occasion showed you really cared… now you're just slow getting dressed.

- Then, you were praised for standing up for your principles…now you're too stubborn to listen to reason.

- Then, when you bent the rules a bit, you were thinking creatively…now you're not thinking straight.

- Then, when you did something nice because you wanted to, people thanked you for being so thoughtful…now you're advised be careful that you don't over-exert yourself.

- Then, when you hung on to all that stuff, you were reusing and recycling…now you're hoarding.

- Then, when you spent the afternoon loafing, you were enjoying your down-time…now they start suggesting a dozen activities you should get involved in.

- Then, if you fell asleep in front of the TV, it was because you had a rough day…now it's proof that you're getting older.

- Then, when you made a mistake, it was a sign that you're only human…now it's even more proof that you're getting older.

- Then, an evening with nothing to do but watch TV was a dud of an evening…now it's a taste of heaven.

- Then, you walked with your head held high because you had self-confidence…now it's because you're having a hard time getting used to your bifocals.

- Then, you had a pen for writing, a book for reading, a camera for picture-taking, a newspaper for news… now you just have your phone, which you've mis-placed (again).

Help!

One day Grandma called her daughter, a stay-at-home mom. "How are you doing today, dear?" asked Grandma.

"I'm absolutely stressed out!" mom cried. "The kids won't lie down for their naps, the house is a mess, and I just realized I've forgotten to buy some of the ingredients for the main dish I'm fixing for our guests tonight!"

"Oh, honey, let me help," Grandma said. "You sit down with a cup of tea, and I'll be over in a jiffy. I'll watch the kids and tidy up the house while you go to the store to get what you need. Then I can do whatever you want in the kitchen, and you'll be all ready when your company comes over."

"Oh, would you? That would be wonderful!"

"And I'll give Tom a call at the office to see if he can come home an hour or so early to help."

"Tom?" mom asked. "Who's Tom?"

"Why, your husband, of course," replied Grandma, quite confused.

"But my husband's name is Jim." Pause. "Is this Shirley?"

"No, this is Terry."

"Oh, please excuse me," said Grandma. "I thought I was calling my daughter. I must have gotten the wrong number."

'Oh." Pause. "So I guess that means you're not coming over..." mom whimpered.

Tidbits of Truth

It might look like I'm sitting here doing
nothing, but I am actively engaged in waiting
for my problems to go away.

You know you're part of the family when you can
walk into a friend's house and your Wi-Fi
connects automatically.

Don't worry if what people tell you seems
to go in one ear and out the other. If it weren't
supposed to happen, God wouldn't
have given you two ears.

Studies show that cheerful, optimistic
people resist illness more successfully than glum,
angry people. In other words,
a surly bird catches the germ.

Nothing is as embarrassing as watching your
wife do something you told her couldn't be done.

*"When they get older,
some people get extremely difficult.
But I'm going to be different.
I plan to be absolutely impossible."*

The Story of Lot

A grandmother was reading Bible stories to her young granddaughter. When she came to the story of Lot, she read: "God told Lot to take his wife and flee out of the city. They were warned not to look back. But Lot's wife did look back, and she turned into a pillar of salt."

The granddaughter looked thoughtful, and then asked, "Grandma, what happened to the flea?"

Bed Time Prayer

Grandma overheard her little grandson say his bedtime prayers. She quickly realized that he was reciting the alphabet over and over. When she heard his "Amen," she went into his room and asked why he had recited the alphabet so many times.

"Sometimes I can't think of exactly what to tell God," the boy replied, "so I just say all the letters and let God put them together for me."

Problem Solving

While his elderly mother was undergoing a mental health evaluation due to her decreasing ability to solve problems, the man fell into conversation with the receptionist. "So how do you test someone's problem-solving skills?"

"We show them a bathtub filled with water, and then we put a teaspoon and a bucket in front of them and ask them how they would empty the bathtub as quickly as possible."

"Oh, I get it!" exclaimed the man. "A rational person would pick the bucket because it's bigger!"

"No," said the receptionist, "a rational person would pull the plug. When can you come in to see the doctor?"

School Days

Great-great-grandpa: Why, when I was a kid, I had to walk ten miles through a foot of snow to get to school.

Great-grandpa: When I was a kid, I had to walk two miles to the bus stop.

Grandpa: When I was a kid, my parents made me buy my own gas for the car.

Dad, seeing his son in his PJs taking an on-line class: When I was a kid, I had to get up every morning and get dressed.

Street Smarts

A couple arrived at a cab just ahead of another man, and the husband motioned for the man to go ahead and take the cab. As it drove off, his wife said, "Honey, we were there first. Why didn't you stand up for your rights?"

"Because he said he was late for his karate class."

Identity Crisis!

"Since I've retired, I'm having an identity crisis," a husband said to his wife. "I believe I'm a deck of cards." "Not to worry, dear," she replied. "We can deal with it later."

* * *

"Since I've retired, I'm having an identity crisis," a husband said to his wife. "I believe I'm an electric eel." "I'm shocked!" she gasped.

* * *

"Since I've retired, I'm having an identity crisis," a husband said to his wife. "I believe I'm a clock." "Yes, you do seem a little wound up," she replied. "But only time will tell how serious it is."

* * *

"Since I've retired, I'm having an identity crisis," a husband said to his wife. "I believe I'm a camera." "Oh, no!" she gasped. "We need to take care of this in a flash!"

A Rude Awakening

One Sunday after church service, a woman who prided herself on her youthful appearance spotted a familiar face in the crowd gathering at the coffee urn in the parish hall. After thinking where she might have known her, she believed they may have been students together in high school. She approached the woman and said, "Excuse me, but did you go to Cherry Hill High?"

"Yes, I did," replied the woman. "My name is Gloria."

"Gloria! Yes, I remember you! You were in my class!"

Puzzled, Gloria gave the matter some thought for several moments. "What subject did you teach?"

Let's Face It

Little Molly was sitting on her grandfather's lap as he read her a bedtime Bible story. Occasionally she would take her eyes off the book and look intently at her grandfather. Now completely distracted from the story, she reached out and touched the wrinkles on his face. Then she touched her own face. "Grandpa," she said, "did God make you?"

"Yes, He certainly did," Grandpa replied. "He made me a long, long time ago."

"Did God make me, too, Grandpa?"

"You bet He made you!" said Grandpa. "But He made you just a little bit ago."

After touching her grandfather's face and her own again, she announced, "I guess God figured out how to smooth things out by the time He got to me."

Join the Pun!

She started to tell a joke about amnesia, but she forgot the punch line.

Did you hear about the old gent who got hit in the head with a can of soda? He's okay, because it was only a soft drink.

The town had plenty of firewood—it was free for the axing.

When her flashlight batteries died, she found herself delighted.

The most experienced snowplow operators always get the drift of it—you can bank on it!

She was looking high and low for a camou-flage shirt for her grandson, but she couldn't find one.

The old gent who had driven a stick shift all his life wanted to learn about automatic transmission, so he clutched at every word his mechanic told him.

A lot of retired folks relish the fact that they've finally mustard the time to ketchup on their hobbies.

Friends should avoid doing puzzles together for fear it could lead to crosswords.

We couldn't decide between pictures submitted by two illustrators, so we ended up calling it a draw.

She passed her anatomy class by boning up on the facts.

When she decided to specialize in cardiology, she went into it with all her heart.

Her granddaughter's wedding was a really emotional affair. Even the cake was in tiers.

The CEO of a major candy company bought the priciest house in town—he was making a mint.

These days, sleeping comes so naturally to me that I can do it with my eyes closed.

An old farmer tried to show us photos of his wheat fields, but they were all grainy.

A guy thought about buying an origami belt, but then decided it would be a waist of paper.

Hang-gliding at 50 was a thrill, but she ended up soar all over.

I like ducks, but I wish they wouldn't wake me at the quack of dawn.

A patient asked the doctor if his failing hearing was ear replaceable.

When Grandma lost her hearing, she learned sign language. She's finding it pretty handy.

When he tried for the third time to make the fencing team, he was foiled again.

After his lecture, we all thought his theory about earthquakes was on shaky ground.

Our Furry Friends

"He's not what he used to be," the dog owner said to his neighbor. "Used to run after cars up and down the street. Nowadays he just sits on the porch and takes down license numbers."

* * *

A woman took her elderly cat to the vet for his annual checkup. Noticing the animal's sluggishness, the vet asked the woman if the cat could get around okay. "Well, certainly he's not as spry as he used to be," the woman replied, "but he's still able to do a little light mouse work."

* * *

A husband and wife were sitting on the porch looking over their garden. "Oh look," said the husband, "those five rabbits are all in a row and hopping backwards!" "That's called a receding hare line, honey," she said as she looked pointedly at her husband's thinning pate.

Just Browsing

Granddaughter wanted to introduce her grandmother to the internet. They sat down together in front of the screen, and the youngster accessed her favorite search engine. "Grandma," she said, "now you can find out about anything just by typing in a question."

Grandma looked skeptical, but decided to give it a try. "Honey, ask how Aunt Charlotte is doing these days."

New Home

The family had just moved into a new home, and Susie was eager to show her visiting grandmother around. "This is Johnny's room," she announced as they toured the house, "and here's the baby's nursery, and here's my room!" Then, as they passed the master bedroom, she lowered her voice and said solemnly, "we each get a room all to ourselves, but Mommy and Daddy still have to share."

Fifteen years ago,
I had three theories on parenting,
but no kids.

Now I have three kids
and no theories.

All In a Day's Work

A woman was waiting in her doctor's office when suddenly she heard someone yelling, "Typhoid! Tetanus! Flu! Pneumonia! Shingles!" Startled, the woman went up to the receptionist and asked what was going on.

"Oh, that's just Dr. Jones—he likes to call the shots around here."

Had Enough

Mrs. Jones realized that there was a leak in the roof over her kitchen table, so she called a repair man to fix it.

"When did you first notice the leak?" he asked.

"This morning," she said, "when it took me two hours to finish my cup of coffee."

Money's Worth

A man went to the dentist and asked him how much he charged for a tooth extraction. "One hundred dollars," the dentist answered.

"One hundred dollars for two minutes' work?" exclaimed the man.

"Well," said the dentist, "I can do the work very, very slowly."

We're Over It!

At our age, we spend entirely too much time talking about what we aren't able to do anymore. Sure, we might lack the strength, energy, and vitality we had when we were in our high-charged, go-getter, athletic 20s. It's a fact of life for almost all of us, but even those among us who claim that we "accept reality" speak of our past glories in wistful terms. "We're over the hill," we sigh with an unconvincing smile.

What we forget to do is focus on what we are able to do, thanks to the number of candles on our birthday cake and those numerous hills we've managed to skirt around, climb over, or blast through. For example, we are able to:

• Make mistakes without roiling in waves of embarrassment, because we realize that we've all been there, done that more often than we can count, and our real friends love us anyway.

• Believe that there's light at the end of the tunnel (and that it's not usually an oncoming train), because we've endured hardship and helped others through tough times, and we've all come out on the other end.

- Live unconcerned about what other people are thinking about us, because we've discovered that they're probably not judging us at all. And even if they are, so what?

- Feel comfortable in our own skin, because we've come to terms with our appearance, body type, and life circumstances. Though we were told from childhood that real beauty comes from inside, now we know it's true.

- Stop fighting futile battles. We've finally accepted the fact that some things (and people) will never change, or they can't be changed by us.

- Leave behind past hopes and dreams that didn't pan out then and won't now. We can work with things the way they are, and we're free to find the blessings right around us.

Those are the real hills we're over. And many of us can claim we've conquered a few mountains along the way, too. What we're more than able to do now is enjoy the scenery.

Tidbits of Truth

A minor operation is surgery performed
on someone else.

Everyone appreciates the fellow who says he's
going to make a long story short—and does.

Most of us know how to say nothing, but not
everyone knows when to say nothing.

Age is the price we pay for maturity.

You can't depend on your eyes when your
perception is out of focus.

Real friends don't care if your socks
don't match.

You know when people are talking sense—
their opinions match yours.

Sad Story

Three friends, Thelma, Linda, and Elaine, took a road trip to see the sights. On their first stop, they found a small, comfortable hotel where they were given a room on the ninth floor. The next morning, coming back from breakfast at a nearby cafe, they were dismayed to learn that the hotel's one elevator had stopped working.

"We're all in pretty good shape," said Thelma, "so let's take the stairs back up to our room. And to get our minds off the stairs, let's concentrate on something else. For the first three floors, I'll tell jokes. Linda, for the next three floors, you sing songs. Then Elaine, for the last three floors, you tell a sad story." Her friends agreed.

At the fourth floor, Thelma stopped telling jokes and Linda began to sing. At the seventh floor, Linda stopped singing and Elaine began to tell sad stories. "I'll start with my saddest story first," she said. "I left our key card in the car."

Exercise

"At our age, exercise is especially important," a woman said to her lounge-chair-loving friend. "And, believe me, there's nothing better than getting up in the morning, slipping on your sweats, and going for a brisk, four-mile walk."

Her friend said, "Wow, I'm impressed! How long have you been doing that?"

"I start tomorrow."

Popular Prices

A couple went to the box office of a movie theater that advertised Popular Prices. When the man asked for two tickets, the clerk said, "That's twenty-five dollars, please," the man was enraged.

"You call twenty-five dollars for two tickets 'popular'?"

"Well, it's quite popular with the owners."

Retired!

The lens maker called it quits after his job became a real grind.

The landscaper retired at 70 because by that time, he was bushed.

The mountain climber gave it up when he realized he was no longer at his peak.

The baker closed his shop after he had made enough dough.

The banker decided to retire because she lost interest.

The chauffer left his job after he lost his drive.

The auto shop manager, after 25 years on the job, decided to re-tire.

The musician resigned after she was played out.

What's Working...and What's Not

In some businesses, owners or managers call a monthly meeting in which they invite staff members to tell what's working (business-wise), and what's not. "Working" comments are entered on one side of a white board, and "not working" comments (offered by those brave enough to proffer them) land on the other side.

Personal survival in the business world being what it is, the "working" side quickly fills with comments designed to make any CEO's heart swell with pride. The "not working" side might receive a few remarks noting problems so obvious even the higher-ups can't ignore, and the CEO has a well-rehearsed answer to offer.

But now we might have a little more perspective, and we're thinking less about the company and more about life. And when we do, the "what's not working" (life-wise) list grows longer year by year: knees don't bend like they used to...finger joints hurt when a storm's coming in...gray hair is harder and harder to hide...on and on!

So that's why we might need to start giving some attention to the "what's working" side of the chart. Such as: watching the family grow as children marry and have families of their own...cherishing long-time friendships and memories shared...swapping stories with people who have traveled through the same seasons as ourselves, but who have pursued different careers, dreams, interests, and passions, and sometimes in places we have only read about... knowing that hardships can be overcome and that catastrophes are not the end, but most often the beginning of increased wisdom, deepened empathy, and more generous compassion.

What's not working? Honestly, a few things. But they pale in comparison to what's working: a lifetime of living.

"No matter how hard I try to concentrate, my mind keeps wandering. Fortunately, it's never been all that steady, so it won't get far."

LOL!

A woman came to her friend, practically in tears. "My husband is CEO of a wonderful company," the woman sobbed, "and now he wants to give it all up and become an actor!" "Oh, now, don't you worry," her friend said. "It's only a stage he's going through."

* * *

Two women were sitting in an ice cream shop, each enjoying every spoonful of a hot fudge sundae. "So what do you think our chances are of losing weight?" said one. "Slim, very slim," replied the other.

* * *

The dermatologist prescribes ointment for her elderly patient's skin spots. "So this will clear them up?" the patient asks. "It should," the dermatologist replies, "but I never make rash promises."

You know you've reached a certain age when...

- The highway patrol officer who stops you hands you a season ticket.

- You've finally gotten your head together, but your body is starting to fall apart.

- Your late-night TV watching ends at 8.

- Your kids start looking middle-aged.

- You're out shopping and your energy runs out before your money does.

- It takes twice as long in the morning to look half as good.

- You don't bother holding your stomach in, no matter who walks into the room.

- Your secrets are safe with your friends, because they can't remember them.

*Honey, how do you expect me
to remember your birthday
when you don't look a day older
than the day we married?*

How Do You Like Them Apples?

A woman stopped at a roadside fruit stand and picked up a bag of apples. "They're pretty small, aren't they?" she said to the old farmer at the counter as she paid for them.

"Yup," he replied.

As she turned to go back to her car, she took a bite of one of the apples. "They're sour, too!" she exclaimed.

"Yup," he said. "Good thing they're small, ain't it?"

LOL!

The newly retired fellow said, "Doc, my tongue tingles every time I touch it to a cracked walnut wrapped in used toaster-oven aluminum foil. What's wrong with me?"
"I think you have entirely too much time on your hands."

* * *

A husband walked into the living room to find his wife weeping in front of the television. "Why do you sob over imaginary problems of people you've never met?" he asked.
"The same reason you yell when a man you don't know makes a touchdown."

* * *

Wife: You're driving ten miles over the speed limit, dear. Husband: What's wrong with that? We have a guardian angel, don't we?
Wife: Yes, but I think you left him miles behind.

Come Again?

Most of us can remember blurting out the wrong thing at the wrong time, and then trying to repair the damage. Consider the plight of the woman who met a former classmate at their 50th high school reunion.

"So is your husband here with you?" she asked.

"No," came the reply, "he's been in heaven now for two years."

"Oh, I'm so sorry," she said, and then realized how that sounded. "I mean, I'm glad..." she stammered. Completely flustered by this time, she declared, "I mean, I'm surprised..."

Ooops!

Grandson, visiting his grandmother's house, breaks an old vase. Grandma, aghast, sputters, "Do you know how old that vase was? It was from the 18th century!"

"Oh, good," said the boy, much relieved. "At least it wasn't new."

Committee at Work

A congregation wanted to build a new church, so they formed a committee to look into the matter. Several months later, the committee submitted their recommendations:

- With a growing congregation, a new church building is needed.

- The new building is to be located on the site of the present one.

- All usable materials in the old building are to be used in the new building.

- The old building will be used until the new building is completed.

Get the Point?

A man appears before St. Peter at the Pearly Gates. Peter tells the man that he needs 100 points to get into heaven. For every good deed the man has done, he will receive a number of points.

"Okay," the man says. "For a start, I was a faithful husband and a devoted family man."

"Wonderful!" says Peter. "That's worth three points."

The man is surprised at how few points his loyalty has earned, but he proceeds. "I attended church my whole life, sang in the choir, served on the board of directors, and tithed every week."

"Very good," says Peter. "That's one more point."

"Only one!" the man says with a sigh. "How about this—I volunteered to deliver meals to shut-ins, and I did that for twenty years."

"Great! Another point!"

Exasperated the man cries, "At this rate, the only way I will get into heaven is by the grace of God!"

"Correct—come on in!" says Peter as the gates swing wide open.

I used to believe...

- ...that "sticks and stones may break my bones, but words can never hurt me"—until someone dropped an unabridged dictionary on my foot.

- ...that "Have a nice day" was a nice thing to say to someone—until I realized how much pressure I was putting on them.

- ...that I should live each day as if it were my last—until I realized that I'd be completely broke by sunset.

- ...that it didn't matter whether I won or lost—until I lost.

- ...that "there's no fool like an old fool"—until I remembered some of the things I did as a teenager.

*"I'm not bald—
I've just grown taller
than my hair."*

Down on the Farm

A boy was spending the summer with his grandparents who lived in an old farmhouse quite far out in the country. He loved the place—helping Gramps with the chickens, assisting Nana shuck corn and make biscuits, and getting to explore the nearby woods all by himself. But what he hated was having to use the outhouse.

One lazy afternoon, he stood looking at the outhouse. He wondered if he could, with a little push, send it sliding down a nearby slope and into the creek. Since the creek was swollen after a recent rain, he figured that right now would be a good time to try. So he put his shoulder to the structure, and sure enough, it tipped, slid into the creek, and floated away.

That evening, his grandpa asked him to sit down. "Someone pushed the outhouse into the creek today," Gramps said. "Are you by any chance the one who did it?"

The boy hung his head and nodded meekly. "Yes, sir," he admitted, and then added: "My teacher said that when George Washington told the truth about chopping down the cherry tree, he didn't get in trouble."

"Maybe so," replied Gramps sternly, "but George Washington's grandfather wasn't in the cherry tree."

See?

A woman, approaching mid-life, realized that she was having difficulty reading small print and wondered if she needed glasses. When she sat down in the optometrist's chair, the doctor asked, "So, have your eyes ever been checked?"

"No, doctor," she replied, "they've always been blue."

Today

"Remember when we were young marrieds, how we spent money as if there were no tomorrow?" said a husband to his wife.

"I sure do," his wife replied, thinking back fondly to those days.

"Well," hubby announced as he reviewed their bank account. "Tomorrow has arrived."

Q&A

Q: What do you call the last teeth to appear in the mouth?
A: False teeth.

Q: How do angels greet each other?
A: "Halo! Halo!"

Q: What was the longtime carpenter's favorite dessert?
A: Pound cake.

Q: What two words are guaranteed to stop any argument?
A: "I agree."

Q: If two's company and three's a crowd, what's four and five?
A. Nine.

Q: How many sheep do you need to make a sweater?
A: Don't know—you'll have to ask a sheep that knits.

As Soon As.....

I decide to make myself a cup of tea, but on my way to the kitchen, I look out the front window and see that I've forgotten to turn off the lawn sprinkler. So I'll make the tea.

As soon as I shut off the sprinkler. Heading outside, I notice that the grandkids have left handprints on the glass storm door. I'll get to the sprinkler,

As soon as I wipe the storm door. Going back inside to get a towel and glass cleaner, I find that someone has moved the glass cleaner from the broom closet. I'll wipe the storm door,

As soon as I find the glass cleaner. Searching through the house, I discover I forgot to make the bed this morning. I'll track down the glass cleaner,

As soon as I make the bed. Just as I start pulling up the blankets, it dawns on me that I left the front door open and the cat could get out. I'll finish the bed...

As soon as I find the cat. So I go outside and start calling the cat, and a neighbor comes over and offers to help. So by the end of the afternoon, no tea is made, the sprinkler is still running, the glass door is still smeared, the glass cleaner has not been located, the bed remains unmade...and the cat is found sound asleep on the living room sofa.

How come I can't get anything done?

"Don't let aging get you down because it's simply too darn hard to get back up."

"I'd like to open a joint account with someone who has a lot of money."

Clearly Defined

Clothes dryer: An appliance designed to eat socks.

Garage sale: A good way to distribute all the stuff in your garage to dozens of other garages all over town.

Classic novel: A book everyone should read, but few actually have.

Synonym: A word you use instead of the one you have trouble pronouncing.

Left speechless: Term we use when about to describe, in excruciating detail, the whole incident.

LOL!

"My children are at an absolutely perfect age,"
said a woman to her friend. "They're too old to
get me up at night, but too young
to drive the car."

* * *

"You are what you eat," a wife reminded her
husband as they perused the menu.
"Great!" replied her husband. "Let's both
order something rich!"

* * *

Two satellite dishes in adjoining backyards
fell in love and got married. Though the
ceremony wasn't much to speak of,
the reception was marvelous.

* * *

I joined an aerobics exercise class for seniors.
I jumped, bent, twisted, and gyrated
for an hour. But by the time I got my leotard on,
the class was all over.

All in a Name

Two longtime friends were chatting when suddenly one said to the other, "I'm really embarrassed to have to ask, but would you please tell me your name again?"

"What?" cried her friend. "We've known each other for years, and you're asking me my name?"

"I'm really sorry," said the woman, "but I just can't remember. Please tell me again."

Silence. Then her friend finally said, "So, how soon do you need to know?"

**"We both went into
the dryer together,
but I came out alone!"**

Adages and Afterthoughts

A penny saved...
makes no difference at all.

If at first you don't succeed...
call it version 1.0.

If you can't stand the heat...
lie in a hammock with an ice-cold soda.

Look before you...
run into a flagpole.

You can't teach an old dog new...
phone apps.

A journey of a thousand miles...
begins when the guy at the wheel claims
he knows a shortcut.

Up the Ante

A husband and wife both talk in their sleep. He loves to play golf, and she loves going to auctions.

One night, during a deep sleep, the husband yells, "Fore!"

The wife, also sound asleep, shouts, "Four-fifty!"

Full Service

A fellow puts his coins in a coffee vending machine, then watches helplessly as the cup fails to drop and the nozzle squirts his beverage down the drain. "Well, that's real automation," he exclaims to the next guy in line. "This machine not only pours coffee, but drinks it for you!"

Ouch!

A pastor arrived at church with a cut on his face. "What happened, Pastor?" asked one of the elderly parishioners.

"I cut myself shaving this morning because I was thinking about my sermon."

"Well, Pastor," said the parishioner, "next Sunday you might want to cut your sermon and concentrate on your shaving."

You've reached a certain age when...

- You have found that the best thing to make for the big, multi-generational family meal is reservations.

- You wake up early even when you haven't set the alarm.

- You refuse to admit you're suffering from insanity, because in fact you're enjoying every minute of it.

- You start using phrases your mother used to use, and you promised yourself you'd never say.

- You hear people say how young you look for your age.

- You want to inform stiletto-wearing young ladies that they are ruining their posture.

- Someone admires your alligator shoes, but you're barefoot.

- You don't recognize any of the "classic" pop songs anymore.

- You believe speed limits should be lowered.

- You have to scroll way down on a web page to find the year you were born.

- You know you've been there and done that, but can't quite recall what it was.

- You spot a gray hair on your adult-child's head.

We Can Get It for You

It was the first day on the job for the young manager of a big-box retail store. As he was walking around the floor, he stopped to hear the conversation between a longtime stocker and a customer. "No, we haven't had that in quite a while," the stocker said, "and I doubt we'll be getting it again anytime soon."

Horrified, the manager stepped in and assured the costumer that the store would have what she wanted in just a few days. He thanked her for her business and said he hoped she'd drop by again soon.

After the customer walked away, the manager reprimanded the stocker for saying that they were out of a product, because he could order anything and have it on the shelves within the week. "So what was it that she wanted?" he asked, picking up his order form. "Rain."

LOL!

"I'm really worried about my insomnia,"
he said with a yawn. "Well, don't lose any
sleep over it," she replied.

* * *

A husband woke up in the morning, stretched,
and said to his wife: "Honey, I slept like a log!"
"I know, dear," she replied. "I listened to
the sawmill all night long."

* * *

If robots get too powerful, all we need to do is
organize them into committees. Within a week,
they will be utterly ineffective.

* * *

"By the time I realized that my father was right all
along," the mid-lifer told his friend, "my son was
old enough to disagree with everything I said."

*"Archie, have you seen your
little sister anywhere?"*

Early Riser

After the umpteenth "senior moment," Grandma says with a sigh, "I just don't know how it is I can make so many mistakes in one day."

Granddaughter says, "Because, like, you got up early?"

Don't Overdo It

A longtime employee asked his boss for Friday off so he and his wife could celebrate their twenty-fifth wedding anniversary.

"Well, all right," the boss growled, "but I don't intend to put up with this every twenty-five years, you know."

Worth Noting

Age is an issue of mind over matter.
If you don't mind, it doesn't matter.
Mark Twain

To keep the heart unwrinkled,
to be hopeful, kindly, cheerful, reverent—
that is to triumph over old age.
Thomas Bailey Aldrich

To me, old age is always
15 years older than I am.
Francis Bacon

It's not how old you are,
it's how you are old.
Jules Renard

Morning Commute

Grandma stayed with her grandson so his parents could take a short vacation. On the first morning, the boy missed his school bus, so Grandma had to drive him. Since she didn't know the way, she asked her grandson to direct her. They circled block after block for 20 minutes before arriving at the school. Realizing they weren't far from the boy's house, Grandma asked why he had led her around in circles.

"Grandma, that's the way the school bus goes, and it's the only way I know."

Tidbits of Truth

The only thing more admirable than being
able to speak several languages is being
able to keep your mouth shut in one.

We never learned anything by doing
it right the first time.

The severity of the itch is inversely
proportional to the length of the reach.

Those who take the road less traveled
can expect a lot of auto repair bills.

You can go almost anywhere you want
if you look serious, wear a lab coat,
and carry a laptop.

It's not a good idea to wave to a friend
at an auction.

A sure-fired cure for insomnia
is plenty of sleep.

We're always open to others' advice—
unless it interferes with our plans.

Those who waste time have yet to
discover the value of life.

The other line always moves faster
until you get in it.

The probability of being watched is in
direct proportion to the stupidity of the act.

Try It

After a lifetime of avoiding exercise, Pete is urged by his doctor to join a gym. So he decides to give it a try. The trainer takes him around to see the various exercise machines, and Pete stops at the treadmill, figuring this will be an easy way to prove what great shape he's in. "I'll set it for ten minutes," the trainer tells him, "and if you want to go longer, just press the button for another ten minutes."

"Should be a cinch," Pete says as he steps on the treadmill and starts walking, faster and faster as the seconds tick away. Within two minutes, however, he's gasping for breath. Red faced and sweating, he jumps off the machine and plops himself down on a bench next to another senior and wheezes, "Man, I lasted barely a couple minutes on that thing!"

The other fellow, wiping the sweat off his brow, looks at him and says, "No need to brag about it, pal."

The difference between then and now...

- Then, we tracked the Top 40 hits…
  now we track the price of groceries.

- Then, for a steep price, we ate dinner at
  a fancy restaurant…now, for the same
  price, we eat dinner at home.

- Then, we could climb three flights of
  stairs and think nothing of it…now we
  head straight to the elevator.

- Then, people spoke clearly…now it's
  surprising how many people mumble.

- Then, the newspaper was easy to read…
  now they're using smaller print.

- Then, many of us took pride in having
  long hair…now most of us simply long
  for hair.

Join the Pun!

Two older women were comparing their legs. One said to the other, "My veins are more prominent than yours, but yours come varicose."

* * *

A woman went to the butcher and hoped to get some venison, but the price was just too deer.

* * *

A couple bought a state-of-the-art TV, but then realized they hadn't the remotest idea how to turn it on.

* * *

Yelling at her grandkids through a screen door, Grandma strained her voice.

* * *

If you want to travel from Alaska to Russia, you must get your Bering Strait.

Fish Story

Man approaches a fellow as he's pulling his fishing boat up to the pier. "Catch any fish?" the man asks.

"Sure did," says the fellow. "Caught dozens of 'em just this morning!"

"Well, I guess you haven't figured out that I'm the game warden."

"Well, and I guess you haven't figured out that I'm the biggest liar in the whole county."

LOL!

"I used to have a photographic memory," the octogenarian boasted to his neighbor. "But lately I seem to have run out of film."

* * *

After the patient told his doctor about his memory loss, the doctor promptly asked him to pay in advance.

* * *

"I stopped to think about what you said," a woman told her friend. "Now I can't seem to get started again."

* * *

Then there's the gal who changed her computer password to "Incorrect". That way, whenever she can't remember her password, the computer prompts her with the message, "Your password is incorrect."

Hear?

A husband felt that his wife was becoming hard of hearing, and he wanted to prove it to her. So one evening while she was in the kitchen, he called loudly from the living room: "What's for dinner?" Receiving no answer, he stepped into the dining room and said even louder: "What's for dinner?" Still no answer. Then he walked right up to her and shouted in her ear, "Honey, what's for dinner?"

"For the third time," she shouted back, "we're having hamburger!"

Adages and Afterthoughts

Anything is possible…when you don't know what you're talking about.

Let a smile be your umbrella…and you'll get a mouthful of rain.

He who hesitates is…honked at.

A fellow with both feet planted firmly on the ground is…a guy who can't get his pants off.

If you can smile when things are going wrong…you don't understand what's happening.

When opportunity knocks...don't sit there complaining about the noise.

When nothing is going right...go left.

If at first you don't succeed...reboot.

Silence is golden...but if kids are present, it's suspicious.

Never underestimate the power of... termites.

If the shoe fits...buy several pairs.

Remember When?

Husband and wife are watching TV. "This is the same movie we watched last week," the husband growls.

"No, it's not," counters the wife.

"It certainly is!" says the husband. "How else would I know exactly how it turns out? And you were sitting right here watching it with me!"

"Huh...did I enjoy the movie?"

"You said you did."

"Well," says the wife as she settles back in her chair, "that's the great thing about being forgetful. You can enjoy things twice over!"

I'm Listening

One Sunday morning during a lengthy sermon, an elderly parishioner fell asleep in the pew. It wasn't until the end of the service and everyone else had left that the preacher sat down next to the man and gave him a gentle nudge. Realizing what had happened, the man kept his eyes closed and head bowed for another several seconds, then slowly lifted his eyes and whispered, "Amen."

Me, Too

Two old friends are taking a stroll through the park. One says, "It's windy today."

"No, it's not," says the other. "It's Thursday."
"Yeah, I'm thirsty, too," the first replies, "let's go for a cup of coffee."

Tidbits of Truth

Some people are wise...
some are otherwise.

Money can buy a house, but it takes love
to have a home.

Those who snore are the ones who fall
asleep first.

If life isn't smiling at you, it's time to give
it a good tickling.

The trouble with aging gracefully is that
you have to age to do it.

Those who are all wrapped up in
themselves are decidedly overdressed.

The miracle medicine is the one that costs
the same as last year.

Worth Noting

When grace is joined with wrinkles,
it is adorable. There is an unspeakable dawn
in happy old age.

Victor Hugo

Wrinkles should merely indicate where the
smiles have been.

Mark Twain

Whenever a man's friends begin to
compliment him about looking young,
he may be sure that they think
he is growing old.

Washington Irving

All would live long, but none would be old.

Benjamin Franklin

Golf—a good walk spoiled.

Mark Twain

Do not judge each day by the harvest you
reap but by the seeds that you plant.

Robert Louis Stevenson

Family History

As you ponder your life's journey so far, you may feel an urge to ensure that the younger generation learns from your hard-won experience and wisdom. You know it would be futile to sit them down for a series of cautionary tales, so you might be drawn to start writing your memoir. This is all well and good, but chances are that you've already conveyed to them a vast amount of practical knowledge about the world—knowledge and know-how passed to you from your parents.

Early on, your parents provided import-ant financial insights—they were not made of money, and money doesn't grow on trees, either. They talked to you about their assets, informing you that they didn't own the elec-tric company (quashing any of your thoughts about eventually inheriting a utility). You may not have known exactly what they did all day, but they let you know (countless times) that they were neither your personal servant nor chauffer.

Your parents made sure you understood the limited abilities of inanimate objects—socks do not pick up themselves. Dirty clothes did not jump into the laundry hamper.

Sometimes, they posed brain teasers, like not to look at them in that tone of voice and a few anatomically doubtful tasks, such as, "Watch your mouth." Well before you could drive, you learned traffic safety—under no circumstances should you and your siblings make it necessary for your mom to stop the car.

Throughout the years, they imparted truths about justice—life isn't fair. You were invited to ponder some of life's deep philosophical questions, such as who you think you are; and what you would do if all your friends were to jump off a cliff. You were offered grammar lessons when they asked you what part of "no" you didn't understand.

Family history, too, was covered. Your parents pointed out that you weren't born in a barn, that they were never bored at your age, and they certainly didn't have it as easy as you when they were growing up.

Yet it wasn't as if they had all the answers! They had questions for you, like, "What kind of grade/music/outfit/attitude is that?" And they waited while you fished for an answer.

At the time, you vowed to yourself you'd never say such things to your kids, but you have to admit that those very words have come out of your mouth. Later on, if not right now, you can sit back, smile, and enjoy the moment when you hear your adult children passing down these same time-honored pieces of wisdom. It's family history in the making!

Weighing In

A wife noticed that her middle-aged husband was trying desperately to hold his stomach in while standing on the scales. "Honey," she said, "that's really not going to help."

"Yes, it is," he replied. "It's the only way I can read the numbers."

Coin Toss

Grandpa was showing his young grandson around Washington, D.C. When they came to the Potomac River, Grandpa mentioned that George Washington is said to have thrown a coin across the water. "That's impossible!" the boy said.

"You've got to realize, Tommy," his Grandpa said, "money went a lot further in those days."

News

One morning a fellow finds two newspapers on his driveway. Seeing the carrier coming back down his street, the fellow shouts, "Hey, you gave me an extra paper!"

"Go ahead and keep it," the carrier yells back, "I'm taking the day off tomorrow."

A helpful little tip from me to you:
Aways keep several get well cards
on the mantle. That way if unexpected
guests arrive they'll think you've
been ill and unable to clean the house!

LOL!

A thoughtful wife is the gal who has pork chops ready
when her husband comes home from a fishing trip.

* * *

She liked to watch auto racing, but she couldn't help but
think that if the drivers had left earlier, they wouldn't
have to go so fast.

* * *

He took an aptitude test to discover what career he was
best suited for, and found out he was perfectly suited
for retirement.

* * *

There are a gazillion products out there that can take
years off your appearance, but not one of them does
anything for a long flight of stairs.

* * *

If everything's coming your way, it's probably because
you're driving on the wrong side of the street.

You've reached a certain age when...

- You look everywhere for your dentures, and find them in your mouth.

- You look everywhere for your cell phone, and discover it's been in your pocket the whole time.

- You look everywhere for your house keys, and find them hanging in the door lock.

- You look everywhere for your sunglasses, and they're perched on top of your head.

- You look everywhere for the holiday decorations you bought at the "Christmas in July" sale, and don't find them...until Easter.

- You look everywhere for the cupcake you bought three days ago...and finally remember you ate it yesterday.

- Your grandkids interview you for their history essay.

- You stop liking loud music.

- You have to ask a ten-year-old to explain the latest craze.

- The sales clerk automatically gives you the senior discount.

- A teenager remarks that you remind him of his grandma.

- You relate to more items in antique shops than in big-box stores.

- Your favorite fashions are trendy… again…and again.

LOL!

You could reach a point later in life where you've learned everything. Your challenge then will be to remember it.

* * *

Perhaps living in the past isn't such a bad idea—things were a lot cheaper then.

* * *

Then there's the gal who's been pressing 50 for so long that she's pleated.

* * *

A good way to look younger is to hang out with people much older than yourself.

* * *

The older generation thought nothing of getting up at 5 a.m. every morning to get to work. Funny thing: The younger generation doesn't think much of it, either.

Senior Moments

Three gals were talking about aging. One said, "I have these senior moments all the time. Why, just this morning I was in the middle of the kitchen holding a loaf of bread, and I couldn't remember whether I was on my way to the toaster or the breadbox."

"That's nothing," the second said. "This morning I stopped in the middle of the stairway and couldn't remember whether I was going up or coming down."

"I'm certainly glad I don't have problems like that—knock on wood," the third said as she tapped on the table. "Oh, excuse me while I go see who's at the door!"

Just Sayin'

Wife: Honey, do you have a good memory
for faces?
Husband: Yes, I believe I do.
Wife: That's good, because I just broke your
shaving mirror.

Doctor: In what ways does your condition
affect your memory?
Patient: I forget.
Doctor: You forget? Can you give me an
example of something you've forgotten?

Patient: Doctor, after my operation, will
I be able to play a good game of golf?
Doctor: No reason why not.
Patient: Great! Because I sure don't play very
well now.

Boy: Grandma, how old are you?
Grandma: Thirty-nine and holding.
Boy: Grandma, how old would you be
if you let go?

Girl skunk: Your jokes aren't funny!
Boy skunk: Are too!
Girl skunk: No, your jokes really stink!

Don't Ask Me

A fellow was sitting on his front porch when a young man carrying a laptop approached him. "Whatcha selling?" the fellow asked.

"I'm not selling anything, sir" the young man replied. "I'm a census taker."

"A what?"

"A census taker. We're trying to find out how many people live in the United States."

"Well, I'm sorry I can't help you, young man," the fellow said, "because, I have no idea."

Smart Girl

Two girls are walking in the park one day when they hear a voice call out, "Hey, girls, down here!" They stop, look down, and see a frog by the side of the pond. The frog says, "If you kiss me, I'll turn you into a glamorous actress, and you'll be rich and famous!"

One of the girls reaches down and grabs the frog and puts it in her pocket.

"Why did you do that?" says her friend. "Why didn't you kiss her?"

She replies, "Because anyone knows that a talking frog is worth a lot more than a glamorous actress any day!"

Q&A

Q: What goes up but doesn't come down?
A: Your age!

Q: Why did the old fellow keep getting back on his bike every time he fell off?
A: Because he was a firm believer in recycling.

Q: When does an elephant charge?
A: When he runs out of cash!

Q: How can you know when you look old?
A: When you go to an antiques auction and three people bid on you.

Q: When is a 50-year-old's bedtime?
A: About three hours after he falls asleep in his chair.

Q: What's the best thing about going to college late in life?
A: If you cut classes, no one's going to call your parents.

Q: Where are seniors most happy to admit their age?

A: At the checkout counter whenever there's a 10% discount.

Q: Why are older parents reluctant to clean out their basement, attic, or garage?

A: Because the minute they do, their adult kids will want to store stuff there.

Q: What's the difference between a cat and a comma?

A: A cat is a critter with claws at the end of its paws, and a comma is a pause at the end of a clause.

Q: What did the balding man say when he received a comb for a present?

A: "Thanks! I'll never part with this."

Tidbits of Truth

Be true to your teeth,
or they will be false to you.

It's true that you're only young once,
but you can be immature forever.

Always go that extra mile, especially when
what you want is a mile away.

Life not only begins at forty,
but it also starts to show.

Remember, you don't have to know
everything—just the web address
of someone who does.

You know you're driving an old car
when you park in front of a museum
and they tow it inside.

There are two sides to every argument—
except the one you're in.

***Sometimes you're the
windshield and sometimes you're...
well, you know.***

We Can Take It!

If we're over 40, a lot of people think we don't like change. Phooey! Sure, we might undergo bouts of nostalgia when we start remembering when, as kids, we were able to run around foot-loose and fancy-free. Even if that was not our reality—doesn't matter. If we didn't live behind a white picket fence, someone we know did, or someone we heard about from a friend of a friend.

But let's admit it—it's pretty much gone, except on TV reruns of classic sitcoms where kids were raised in a rural town where no problems arose that couldn't be solved in the space of 30 minutes. In real life, the past never offered picture-postcard perfection. Things changed then and continue to change now—always have, always will as long as the world keeps spinning.

What those of us who have lived a number of decades are really saying about change is that there are some changes we like, and others we don't like. We want to pick and choose. Say, cafeteria-style.

In the cafeteria of changes, some among us might grab for a healthy, balanced good-and-bad-change meal. But most of us would head straight to the good-change dessert line. Indulge the sweet tooth. Never mind vegetables (never liked 'em anyway) or meat and potatoes (save the calories for a couple slices of pie). Yet, like the kid who eats a box of cookies all by himself, we'd soon find ourselves feeling—well, not so happy.

There's something better than picking the change we want, and that's embracing the change that happens. Exploring it. Listening to it. True: not all changes will work for us—even younger folk have to cope with turns of events that aren't to their liking. But there's one thing we know for sure, because we have a lot of change to look back on—change brings good things and bad things. Ups and downs. Highs and lows. Cherries and pits. And over the years, we have coped in some way with all of them.

Change. It's not always easy, not always pleasant, but often means growth, opportunity, and fulfillment...and it's better than a continuous diet of chocolate chip cookies (maybe).

The Visitor

A dentist was working late one night when a man walked in the door. "Excuse me, but I need your help. I think I'm a moth."

"I'm a dentist. It sounds to me like you need a psychiatrist," the dentist said.

"Yes, I know."

"Then why did you come in here?"

The man replied, "Because the light was on."

At the Movies

A theater patron was watching a movie when two friends entered and plopped themselves in the seats directly in front of her. Immediately the two friends commenced a long, drawn-out conversation. After several minutes of this, the woman tapped one of her noisy neighbors on the shoulder and said, "Excuse me, but I can't hear."

"I should hope not!" the chatterer sharply replied. "This is a private conversation!"

Clearly Defined

File cabinet...a place where you can lose
things in alphabetical order.

Tropical resort...place you spend $250 a day
to stay at during the winter so you can bask
in the 95 degree heat that you complained
about all summer.

Gray hair...what a lot of people dye over.

Reality...where some people visit,
but don't stay long.

Tainted money...cash that 'taint yours.

Keychain...trinket that lets you lose all your
keys at once instead of one at a time.

Hair stylist...someone who fixes your hair in
a way that you can never manage to
duplicate at home.

**When it comes to the lawn,
my dad is a perfectionist—
every blade of grass is a foot high.**

Just for Pun

Stop Arguing! by Xavier Breath

I Lost My Balance by Eileen Dover and Phil Down

Desert Crossing by I. Rhoda Camel

Gourmet Eating by Ima Cook

The Joy of Archery by Beau N. Arrow

Slow Down! by Terry A. While

All About Mosquito Netting by I. Itch

On Bathing Your Cat by Claude Hands

Irish Heart Surgery by Angie O'Plasty

Backyard Gardening by Daisy Flowers

It's Morning!

One morning a mother knocked on her son's bedroom door. "Get up and get dressed!" she shouted. "It's time to go to school!"

"Aw, Mom, I really don't want to go today," came the reply.

"Now you give me two good reasons you don't want to go," Mom said.

"Because the kids don't like me, and the teachers don't like me, either!"

"Those aren't good reasons. Now get up and get dressed."

"So give me two good reasons why I should go to school."

"Number one, you're 45 years old. And number two, you're the principal!"

Be Careful!
There could come a time when...

- A hot water bottle has a permanent place among your bed pillows.

- Your contact list grows exponentially with names beginning with "Dr."

- You knees buckle, but your belt won't.

- You feel an overwhelming urge to move to Florida and take up golf.

- You sit in a rocking chair but can't get it going.

- Your back goes out more often than you do.

- You can get most of your shopping done at the pharmacy.

Getting Some Exercise

Husband and wife decided they wanted to get more exercise, so they bought an exercise machine and set it up in the basement. After several months, both admitted that they hadn't yet used the machine, so they moved it to their bedroom. After another few months, the machine had not been used. Finally they moved it into the living room, thinking that the prominent location would remind them to use it. Weeks later, when a friend asked if the machine they had bought was helping them get more exercise, the wife enthusiastically said, "Absolutely!" She went on to explain: "It's so in the way, that every time we go into the living room, we have to walk around it!"

Tidbits of Truth

Experience is a wonderful thing. It
enables you to recognize a mistake when you
make it again.

It's easy to meet expenses...
everywhere you go, there they are!

The fewer words we speak,
the fewer we're obliged to eat.

Never complain about the weather—without it,
we'd have a hard time starting a conversation.

Some people dream of doing what they love...
others wake up and do it.

Social tact is the ability to make visitors feel at
home even when you wish they were.

The quickest and least expensive way to have
your family tree thoroughly
researched is to run for public office.

Let's Lunch

Three girlfriends were turning 50 the same month, and they wanted to celebrate together. They decided to meet for lunch at the Mountaintop Café because it was quite trendy and the servers there were all very handsome. On the big day, the ladies had so much fun at the Café that they vowed to make it a tradition—every ten years, they would have a birthday get-together. As they approached their 60th birthdays, they discussed where to meet for lunch, and opted for the Mountaintop Café because the food was good and the servers were cute.

When their 70th birthdays rolled around, they again talked about their various choices of venue. Finally they chose the Mountaintop Café because it wasn't too noisy there, the view was stunning, and the servers were such sweet kids.

Ten years later, in view of their 80th birthdays, they again selected the Mountaintop Café because it was wheelchair accessible, had a good selection of heart-healthy meals, and the servers were kind and helpful.

When it came time to plan their 90th birthday celebration, the friends wanted to try something new. They met at the Mountaintop Café, because no one could remember going there before.

**My wife told me I need
to get in shape, and I told her,
"Round is a shape!"**

In pre-tech days...

- An application was a form you filled out at the employment office.

- A program was something you watched on TV.

- A web was where that big, fat, scary garden spider lived.

- Loss of memory was something that happened to elderly neighbors.

- A hard drive is how your parents describe the cross-country road trip during which you whined, "Are we there yet?" every 30 minutes.

- A cursor used words that would get you in a lot of trouble if you were to repeat them.

- A keyboard was what you used when you learned to play "Twinkle, Twinkle Little Star" on the piano.

- Logic was what you tried to use to convince your parents that you had good reasons for arriving home two hours after midnight.

- CDs were financial products your parents bought at the bank.

- Data was personal information you kept in a cardboard box labeled Stuff.

- A printer was someone who worked at the newspaper office downtown.

- A phone was just a phone...and it was connected to the wall, not to you.

- A disc was a plastic plate that you threw and your collie caught.

- A mouse was what made your mom leap on a kitchen chair and scream.

Strolling Along

A tourist was out for a walk in the country and suddenly realized that he had traveled quite a distance from where he had come. Turning around, he noticed a farmer working in his field. "Say, how long will it take me to get back into town?"

The farmer looked up, but didn't answer, so the man shrugged and continued on his way. After a few minutes, he heard the farmer yell, "About thirty minutes, mister!"

Turning around, the man said, "Thanks. But why didn't you tell me that when I first asked you?"

"Well," the farmer replied, "I didn't know how fast you could walk."

Clearly Defined

Etc.: What we say when we know there's more to the story, but we can't think of it at the moment.

Grocery list: What we spend an hour creating and then forget to take to the store.

Confidential information: Tidbits we tell one person at a time.

Tomorrow: When we'll do the chores we had planned for today.

Wrinkles: What other people have; we have smile lines.

Egotist: Someone who's always me-deep in conversation.

Successful acupuncture: A jab well done.

Adages and Afterthoughts

Early to bed and early to rise...
means you're probably retired.

You're never too old to...
wear more bling.

A rolling stone...
could trip you and make you fall down.

Stop and smell the...
chocolate chip cookies.

Two heads...
would mean twice as many wrinkles.

The pen is...
rarely picked up anymore.

When the going gets tough...
it might be because your knee joints ache.

**I can't be out of money—
I still have some checks left!**

His Midlife Crisis-1

When he turned 45, Bob decided he'd do what he had been dreaming of doing for a long time—he'd buy a boat. Despite his wife's objections, he bought one, docked it at a nearby marina, and then took his wife out to see it.

"Isn't it gorgeous, honey?" he gushed. Hearing no response and hoping to generate enthusiasm, he said, "Say, why don't you pick out a name for her?"

"Sure," his wife replied, "I'll be happy to do that."

The next weekend when her husband went to the dock, this is the name he saw painted on the side of his boat: For Sale.

His Midlife Crisis-2

Bill had always wanted a motorcycle, and on his 50th birthday, he bought one for himself. On his maiden run, he pulled onto the highway and thoroughly enjoyed the thrill of the ride. Then after a few miles, he sidled up to a car and yelled at the driver, "Hey, buddy, ever driven a motorcycle?"

"No, I haven't," the driver shouted back, and the biker sped on. He spotted another car, positioned himself next to it and yelled, "Hey, buddy, ever driven a motorcycle?"

"No, I haven't," the driver shouted back, and the biker sped on. Suddenly the biker approached a sharp curve, swerved into a ditch, and fell off his motorcycle into the grass. A motorist stopped, ran to the scene, and helped the stunned biker get back up on his feet.

The biker said, "You ever driven a motorcycle?"

"Sure," the good Samaritan replied, "driven one for years."

"Then tell me, where are the brakes?"

All That Stuff

"You can't have everything." We know this, and frankly, we're relieved. And it's not always because we've attained the spiritual maturity to realize that stuff brings short-lived happiness at best, but because we've come to a very practical realization: When it comes to downsizing, less is better.

Ask anyone who is thinking about swapping the old rambling, multi-story homestead for a small, modern, two-bedroom ranch. No stairs—yay! Easy to clean—yay! Postage-stamp size yard—yay! What's the hold-back? It's the thought of going through all those trunks, boxes, and closets stacked in the basement, in the attic, and in the garage.

Old toys have been saved for the day grandchildren come over and squeal with delight over getting to play with mom or dad's dollhouse or trainset. But chances are they stare in wonder that such relics could actually have amused their parents, and they go back to what's really fun—the latest phone app. Nonetheless, our dream lives on, and the toy box stays.

Then there are the pictures, plates, bowls, vases, and knick-knacks that our parents left us. But they never did fit our color scheme or complement our décor. That was their stuff, and we wanted new stuff. So now we're storing boxes of our parents' stuff, plus all the stuff we have accumulated over the years, none containing stuff we could fit into a smaller home, much less contribute to a more carefree lifestyle.

What else? Decades worth of vacation souvenirs. Awards, trophies, and commemorative gifts from schools, employers, and community groups. Yellowed tax documents, bank statements, and utility bills. Clothes that made us feel so cool back then, but we wouldn't wear today on a dare. Desks, chairs, and dressers shrouded in years of dust.

Oh, and there's the stack of plastic tubs chockfull of stuff the kids left, and we figured they'd come and get them once they got settled. Nope. Hopes of anyone coming to take the tubs were dashed when the young families became the proud owners of places no bigger than a garden shed.

How about the garage? A mountain of leftover screws and nails from various assemble-it-yourself furniture projects. Half-empty spools of cord, wire, and twine. An assortment of hooks and hinges and metal thingamajigs that seem to have multiplied on the workbench when we weren't looking.

Lawn mowers. Power tools. Barbells. Bicycles. Bins of Christmas garland, wreathes, ribbons, bells, and illuminated characters sufficient to decorate Main Street.

And that's only what we have now! It doesn't include what we have ever wanted or wished for or tried to get or owned at one time and discarded. "You can't have everything"— thank goodness!

LOL!

A house right next to the highway would be
convenient, except that you would have
to be going 65 miles an hour just to
get out of your garage.

* * *

The trouble with being punctual is that there's no
one around to appreciate it.

* * *

His golf game was so bad that if he grew
tomatoes, they'd come up sliced.

* * *

Baby camel woke up his parents at 3 a.m.
"Mommy, Daddy, I need a drink of water!"
"Another one already?" Mom says. "That's the
second glass this month!"

* * *

There are two kinds of electronic devices on the
market these days: those that waste your time,
and those that waste your time faster.

The Children of Israel

Grandpa was reading a Bible story to his granddaughter. He told her how Moses led the Children of Israel out of Egypt, how they crossed the Red Sea, and how the Children of Israel at last entered the Promised Land. When he finished, his granddaughter thought a minute and then said, "What I'd like to know is, what were the grownups doing all that time?"

The Sunday Paper

"You didn't deliver my Sunday paper this morning!" a caller yelled to the newspaper's customer service agent.

"Ma'am," the agent replied, "this is only Saturday. The Sunday paper will be delivered to your home tomorrow morning, on Sunday."

There was a pause on the line. "Well," the caller said sheepishly, "I guess that tells me why I was the only one at church today."

It's Morning!

Two neighbors were taking a break from their yard work when they got into a discussion about animal behavior. "Dogs are the most loyal critters I can think of," claimed one, "and for sure the mule is the most stubborn animal on God's green earth."

"That's true," said the other, "and I say geese are by far the friendliest."

"How so?"

"Well, whenever I'm out mowin' the lawn and a skein of 'em flies by, every single one of 'em geese honks and waves!"

How come...

- ...the minute you dip your hands in warm, soapy water, your nose runs?

- ...a month after the warranty expires, the appliance stops working?

- ...when you have extra time on your hands, you spend it wondering what it was you must have forgotten to do?

- ...the probability that tomato sauce will splatter on your placemats is in direct proportion to the whiteness of the placemats?

- ...when you finally get rid of something that's been in the attic for years, you need it the next day?

- ...when it looks simple, it never is?

- ...when you want to unlock the door but have only one hand free, your house key is in the opposite pocket?

- …your insurance covers everything except what has really happened?

- …when you have one problem solved satisfactorily, two more take its place?

- …the chance of rain spikes dramatically when you've parked at the end of the lot and forgotten your umbrella?

- …another shopper is always standing right in front of the shelf with the product you want to buy?

- …the only snack you really like in the vending machine is gone?

- …when you're late for an appointment, you hit every intersection just as the light turns red?

- …the chances of locking your keys in the car increases exponentially on the hottest/coldest/snowiest/rainiest day of the year?

- …the one time you arrive late for a doctor's appointment, the doctor is early?

Fond Memories

A woman was showing her friend a locket containing a lock of her husband's hair. Shocked, her friend gasped, "I'm so sorry! I had no idea he had passed."

"Oh, he is quite alive," her friend replied, "but his hair is long gone."

Time Tells

Having just turned 40, a woman stood in front of a mirror and scrutinized her appearance for any sign of aging. "Eeeek!" she screamed when she discovered a streak of gray hair framing her face. "Honey, just look at this!" she said to her husband as she pointed to her face.

"Huh?" he replied glancing up from the TV. "You mean the wrinkles?"

Adages and Afterthoughts

Actions speak louder...
when your knees are creaky.

Those who laugh last...
didn't get it the first time.

An idle mind is...
necessary for an afternoon nap.

Two wrongs...
are generally only the beginning
of a huge problem.

Honesty is...
easier than trying to remember
something you made up yesterday.

If you want it done right...
and if it has to do with an electronic device,
ask a ten-year-old.

LOL!

"Didn't you see that stop sign?" the trooper asked the driver. "Sure, but at my age, I'm smart enough not to believe everything I read."

* * *

Laughter is the best medicine. But if you're laughing when nothing is funny, you should opt for the medicine.

* * *

"I've changed my mind," she declared.
"Good," he replied.
"I hope this one works better for you."

* * *

A woman went to the gym to sign up for a beginner's body-firming exercise class. "How flexible are you?" asked the instructor. "For one thing," she said, "I can't do Wednesdays."

* * *

A woman went to a doggie boutique and asked to see holiday sweaters for her Chihuahua. When the sales assistant recommended bringing the dog in, the customer replied, "Oh, I don't want to do that, dear. This is a surprise."

The Big Diet

A couple decided they needed to lose weight, so they embarked on a dietary program that had recipes for three meals a day for 30 days. After a week of faithfully following the plan, they were delighted to discover that the meals were delicious and, best of all, they weren't hungry in the least. At the end of the month, however, they discovered to their horror that they had both gained five pounds. Only then did they reread each recipe and noticed the fine print: Serves 4.

In the Event of an Emergency

Mom was helping her young daughter memorize her home address. Though the street name posed no problem, the girl kept mixing up the house numbers. "Honey," Mom prompted, "if there were a fire at our house, what would you tell them when you called 911?"

"I would say, 'Come to Cherry Street and look for the house that's on fire.'"

*Wrinkles should
merely indicate
where smiles
have been.*
Mark Twain